Freeing our Goddance
Poems & Meanderings for Heart & Soul

Judy A. Guadalupe

Cover Artwork
Nina Ayzenberg

Published by:
Judy Guadalupe
Create Space
www.judyguadalupe.com
www.createspace.com
ISBN:13: 978-1493746842

Cover Design by Nina Ayzenberg
Editor: Debbie Caldwell

Passionate, with longing in mine eyes,
Searching wide, and seeking nights and days,
Lo' I beheld the Truthful One, the Wise,
Here in mine own House to fill my gaze.
Lalla (Lalleshawri) 1355

Dedication

This book is dedicated to the earth angels who have walked closest beside me. My family - Isaiah, Elijah, Rhia and Krishna, and our 17-year-old 4-legged angel, Ananda: May you always know your magnificence and feel forever deeply loved and cherished. The most remarkable blessing of this life of mine, for which I am eternally grateful, has been walking and waking by your sides. Thank you.

For those who have supported me from my birth -- my parents, Jo-Ann and Jack, and our ancestors; my 12 siblings; my godmother Julie; and the forty something ever-growing family members who all always love each other no matter what, a "rare family" (see poem within): You are each an inspiration and light by whom all are blessed. As far away as I may seem, you always live in my heart. Thank you.

For our two "newest" full angels whose presence upon our planet was/is a phenomenal blessing beyond measure to me, their families and everyone who knew them: Now you have your full wings, and are an expanded presence of love for all, Sr. Bernadette McCann and Chris Miller.

For my soul family all over the planet: How I love our connectedness beyond time and space; realizing this together is pure joy. You are an indelible part of my heart.

And for all of you who have encouraged me to get these writings in print: Thank you. I so appreciate you. I am forever delighted by the continued synchronistic meetings upon our sacred Gaia; the miraculous reunions are beyond what I could have imagined! And I imagine love continuing to discover itself everywhere.

With deep gratitude and love.

~ If You Don't Stop That ~
I used to live in a cramped house with confusion and pain.
But then I met the Friend and started getting drunk and singing all night.
Confusion and pain started acting nasty, making threats, with talk like this,
"If you don't stop 'that'---- All that fun---- We're leaving."
Hafiz 1320

Introduction

For many years, I have found something to write upon, quietly in journals or words spilling onto small pieces of paper or envelopes here and there, random poems and inspirations birthed in life's moments of inspiration and contrast. The offering of my Evenings of Inspiration, Laughter and Love allowed me to publicly share my writings for the first time and now, delightedly, they are in print.

Please hold loosely any strict idea of proper, literary form or style in my writer's expression. These poems are the meanderings of my heart and soul in a freestyle word-dance. The writings may seem to appear without exact order or reason, a bit like life can feel at times. Allow the words to call you, open to any page and receive.

A lover of many poets and writers, I am especially grateful to the master seers whose writings have infused me with love, and invoked from within me, through word, what my mind cannot know.

Hafiz. (1320-1389) words to me are a pure invitation of melting into the Beloved. He is one poet who seems to swim in my very veins and ignite my soul. His transmission, invitation, love, ecstatic humor; these mystical, cosmic and sublime words enter deeply my heart and move my pen through grace, making quite tangible the privilege of knowing that yes I accept the inner invitation to be the mother, the lover, the daughter of Hafiz. I pray words falling from my pen may bring a smile to your heart and inspire deep love and delight in Being.

What is the Root of all these worlds?
One thing: love.
But a love so deep and sweet ~
It needed to express itself with scents, sounds, colors
that never before existed.
Hafiz

Prologue

One day as I was writing, I saw that where I had intended the word *guidance*, *goddance* had appeared instead. My body felt chills and a heart-smile graced my lips -- you know, it was one of those charges you get when something feels aligned and inspired. I felt the beauty of the perception that each of us is a god**dancer**, each of us part of the One and yet, unique, whole, sovereign. I thought of the many teachings across time and space that have guided us to "know thyself," to know that what we search for is within, that "I and the Father are one," and that there is available to us now a middle way, a neutrality, a "peace that passeth all understanding," a complete inner alignment with Source. It was as if all my lifetimes of seeking, of knowing, of experiencing contrast and apparent separation merged into this present moment where all is Now.

I have become more acutely aware that what we seek is so. Joy fills me as I see the collective awakening to this realization that, until now, only relatively few had experienced. Thus began the gathering of my poetry for this book, and for the book that I am currently writing called *The Goddance, Dancing Beyond Dogma*, a book that is allowing me to birth my authentic expression -- my god**dance** -- through word. In the moment the word god**dance** emerged on the page, I saw the delicious gift of embodiment and knew that I wanted to use word and humor to inspire this inner awakening and fuel our subsequent collective co-creations and collaborations with the love that we are.

These poems speak to the inherent gift to all beings and our planet of "Freeing Our God**dance**." In the story of humankind's evolution, we have had many turning points where certain people were considered insane for their introductions of new ideas, paradigms, and potentials.. Wooo hooo, we get to be the crazy ones now!
The imaginal cells are the cells within the chrysalis that first vibrate or realize themselves butterflies. This realization and resonance allows all other cells to join on the butterflies flight of freedom in

form. We get to be the imaginal cells that know love as the bottom line and resonate the peace of freedom. Fly free.

Our yearnings to merge, expand, grow, find peace, live freely and passionately, express creatively and serve more fully are our souls' gifts to our transforming world. Coming together, we raise our frequency, accessing yet-unseen options. We serve as mirrors for each other, reminders of our mystic souls' gifts and potentials. We are midwifing each others' fullness. Freeing our god**dance** is not a concept or a hope; it is a surrendering of limitation and fear as the truth of our limitless nature of love emerges.

Your god**dance** is the authentic expression of your magnificence, your impulse of god-love, the unique flavor of you as a being both one with the Source that creates all and present in form for the expansion of All That Is.

As I write, the word "unfathomable" comes to me. *Unfathomable:* "incapable of being fully explored or understood," and "impossible to measure of the extent of;" inscrutable, incomprehensible, enigmatic, indecipherable, impenetrable, obscure, esoteric, mysterious, mystifying, deep, profound. Poetry, art, dance, sound vibrations, scripture, symbols, ancient languages, parables, nature and all her beauty and life, humor, ritual and intimacy speak to us in languages of the mysterious, the unfathomable, the incomprehensible. And we, you and I, get to experience something that gives us an ever-expanding "new" point of reference from which our conscious light can shine. From this unnamable knowing, we are aroused to participate in the world as Love would, co-creating joyful passionate lives in service to All That Is.

I love hearing about the magnificent and diverse ways so many of us are opening and experiencing human unfolding. For some, there is a quiet inward presence of love, for others a roar of outward expression, and for many, a bit of both. As we allow full surrender into this moment, what we see, taste and touch disappears into a soup of existence, merging with All That Is. We fall into knowing and realize the connection and perfection of All, the non-dual basis of all as Divine consciousness, as love and the never-ending impulse of the Divine to know Itself. Now included in our awareness is the realization, the experience, that we have never been separate, there is nowhere to go, nothing happening, nothing to fix, do or realize.

If the unraveling of all identity is not enough to evoke insanity for our conditioned minds, we further embark upon a paradoxical journey. We travel from awareness of our Self as consciousness in the soup of Oneness, to participating fully as co-creators in form to express our unique lives. This is a paradox that commands our hearts, that can be both maddening and deeply, powerfully humbling. As we emerge from this experience of merging "nothingness/ allness" into this (relatively) real experience in form, we may feel stretched to remain with the inner state as we fully participate in our lives. For some, awakening seems to be instantaneous; for most of us, it comes in increments. All of us see our unique emergence moving forth as the impulse of Love, aligned with Source and acting in coherence with all living things.

In the now moment, separation unravels into Oneness, time dissolves and dimensions collapse. Masters and mystics from all walks of life have spoken to us of being one with our Source, God, the Beloved, Creator. This, though, is not a dogmatic understanding or even a learned skill. It is surrender. A death and rebirth. An alignment with the flow of life itself. And realizing that flow is the fierce and gentle promise of your soul in form. There are as many paths to this realization as there are humans, so it is not the *way* that needs to be taught but rather an invitation to surrender that is offered. Many speak of a collective shift in consciousness. Can this be our collective moment?

Andrew Harvey's explanation of our unprecedented collective human experience speaks eloquently of merging into oneness and emerging into full divine expression: "...when the fire of the mystic's passion for God is united with the fire of the activist's passion for justice to form a third fire, which is Divine love and wisdom in action." We are the third fire. And from this place of love in expression, quite naturally our actions could only be on behalf of true freedom and liberty for all.

Your realization and the vibration you become when in alignment with Source is a catalyst to my realization, and on and on. In this consciousness, the perceptual error of separation, and the false notion of contrast as a negative, both lose their power. As Einstein said, "No problem can be solved from the same level of consciousness that created it."

The youth and children and babies carry this awareness. Listen! You and I, and all awakening ones in all their guises, get to play with them in new creations, new paths and places of peace. Look with the eyes of your heart and see who and what shows up.

I love the mystics, poet seers, musicians, people whose expressions portray and invoke the unnameable and undefinable as experience. And I am in awe of those who, from this realization, jump fully into life and become the catalysts for deep, profound evolution in the dimensional reality in which they live. We get to walk side by side as each being's authentic expression of love gifts us with a flavor of the Divine yet to exist!

What brings you home to now and allows you to know fully the love essence within the core nuclei of every atom and molecule of your being? What offers you experience of the mystery of your nature as both One and sovereign? The origin of the word sovereign is said to be an "alteration by influence of reign." For reign, the Thesaurus gives us synonyms of rife and rampant. Look up rife and we find omnipresent! We reign! I'd love for the messages mingled within these poems to evoke from you the ferocious passion and unfathomable peace of the brilliant, rife and rampant, god**dance** that is you.

一九八五

Grace

I long to fill these pages with words that flow forth and fill those
who yearn to feel Your grace as it seeps into them, their cells, their
ever chattering minds, and to allow for a moment, a merging with
You that instantly forgives and frees one from all maya

Poetry

the language of the soul
written by the heart
and its longing
to speak the unspeakable
silence the mind
form the formless
and elicit tears
of joy
for no apparent reason

Love Flows a Promise

Wondering if I just forgot
My promise to the One
That words would flow from me
only as love pours
from the eyes of Mother
as her children come,
tired and alive...
That I would move my pen in service
To delight and ecstasy
Inspiring those who come home
To what is already so...

Intimacy

This morning bird sang to me
I listened until apparent bird and I
Became the song she sang
Meaning was indefinable
(like all really)
Yet we knew the song intimately

Magnificence

Upon the morning dew, brilliant light dances, little crystals of
magnificence appearing momentarily and fully. You, my friend, are
this magnificence. In your momentary experience of YOU, let the
world see, feel, taste and touch your flavors. Not so much in the
doing, simply in your willingness to BE. As you surrender to this
Being within, you become a brilliant bright frequency of refreshing
authentic expression in our world. And the impulse of Spirit through
you - in other words - what you will do with that magnificence - how
you choose to dance your goddance ~ flows effortlessly from your
Self as Love, in service to All That Is.

God's Dance

We are God's dance
And we get to experience that
when we let go
of the thought that says
we are not

A Book by Its Cover

From flower beds
to cardboard houses
In climbing trees and high rise buildings
In toll booths
or with the salesman and his briefcase
In tiny boats at sea
and walking home from church
You'll find them
Now
It does take something on your part
Yes, stop breathe and listen
And as your mother said
"don't judge a book by its cover"
Awakened Ones wear all sorts of disguises
Remember me, Hafiz asks?
A crazy man "they" called me!

Laughing

Hafiz words sometimes fall into me
Like a good wine
and disappear on my tongue
Leaving only a longing
for everyone
to know also this frequency
That creates enough space
between your cells
that moon bumps into your knee
and hits your funny bone
And nothing is left to do
but laugh
Again and again
he's made me laughing!

—උඥුඤ

Squirrel

Squirrel comes sometimes
Yelling at me
Pay attention woman
and have more fun
Or perhaps wildly wags her tail for me
"Play and Sing" she says
"It is the godDance
For which you have come"

Meanderings

Hold the sun in your hands
For as light, light will not burn you
Push past the falsity of your fears
Expand now into the light and love
Allow the mother's love to be born anew in you

You desire not to be good or right, or even loved
You ultimately desire only to express
limitlessly and fully
For love needs not to be loved
And yet as love will attract and experience love
For love like a noun is
Simply is.
Love as some humans live it
has been a verb
Something I give to you
(if, perhaps you behave in a certain way
or give something in return)

Yet, as essence,
you realize yourself as love in expression
From there

~ and the place is only within ~
All expression glorifies love
And forms it into a myriad of delight

If less than love is present
Welcome all the visitors,
pain, grief, hardships that arise
As Rumi says:
"Trust that you are being cleaned out
for some new delight"

Passages Lead Nowhere

Before, I thought,
if I did this ritual or practice right,
if I healed the wounded part of myself,
fixed this money issue
or that relationship
If I just walked through the passageway,
in the right way
then I would arrive...
God came to me as my broken heart and spoke...
"Here too is where I reside
if you feel a need to forgive,
forgive Me...
For being All That Is
Hear me... All That Is
Enter in...
Not with an agenda
of passing through to somewhere else
Simply enter in
and be delighted"

Played by Love

Fullness - emptiness,
huge - tiny,
foreign - native,
aggressive - passive,
deep - shallow,
off - on,
fear - courage,
peace - restlessness,
love - love
There is no opposite of love
Hear this, no opposite of love
When you can drop into love
fully,
in other words, when love swallows you
and you allow it,
finally ~
and you do
and will
Duality merges with wholeness and oneness
in such a fashion
these apparent opposites collide
in a vast brilliant dance
where suns, moons, and planets
have no boundaries

Where the soup of existence
permeates in through and as you
and yet you, in a sense, are no longer.
Love calls more of you, from you,
pours in and out of you as All That Is.
And the unbearableness of the pleasure
keeps making you disappear

When love, when God shows Herself, Himself,
Itself to you in this way
Beware.
Butterflies will speak with you
You will feel the children's laughter in your cells.
Driving may become a challenge ~
for a bit
Walk if you can
Perhaps in the trees,
they will share with you their ancient stories of love

Call upon compassion
as you laugh at the stories that had just a moment ago
seemed so important or devastating
There is nothing more devastating to your story
than the love you truly are
Laugh, Wiggle and Dance my friend
It is the Goddance
that is played by Love
It is the Goddance
for which you have come~!

Silence

In love
I walk these mornings
I feel the barriers
once built around my heart
dissolving
into the silence
The birds' songs
the trees' whispers
my body
becomes the silence itself
And All That Is birthed forth

So Pure This Love

Have you ever touched
something so delicate
that you were hesitant
to fully embrace it
or to believe
you would not cause it harm?

Beyond the tears,
enter in
where you feel
the Beloved you are
fully

Beware
The purity, the tenderness
may melt your life away

Quite welcome
is this disappearance
Love Remains

The Ever Flowing Dance

When I dare
to let go
there is a life force pulse
that carries me

When I merge with it
I disappear into You
and we into All That Is

Being then
nothing
at the dawn,
the impulse of everything
reckons words fallible
or inadequate

The pen calling
an arrow to point
nothingness to everything
and back again

All of it, You are
from no-thing to everything
dancing into and out of
All That Is
Is Love

Moon Moods

As woman,
moon moves me
Taking any idea of stability and security
Or some sort of control
Or idea of having to have it all together
Shakes foundations
So I have nothing left
to stand on
Or believe in
Except life itself
The fullness of moon moves me

Her Ebb and Flow

All the cells in your body
will vibrate with and as
her ebb and flow
as your mind quiets itself enough
May as well help it along
in a practice
or lying naked under Her,
Moon
for She,
this lunar ecstasy,
may disguise itself as lunacy
only to confuse your mind enough
to surrender to the impulse
of love you are

Beloved

She danced
with me so fully
belly started breathing
separately from lungs -
not disconnected really
yet powerful breath its own.
Perhaps
it was primal fear
unraveling itself
into pure excitement
for freedom in our dance
She stole this body's
virginity anew

I can say
reluctance was only present

when thought attempted
to capture, define or judge
the pleasure,
of making love with the moon
and give it form, description

We die
when we imagine
form to be all we are,
You, me, it, them

We miss the mark
when we believe
this merging
into formless the goal

Live love!
and form becomes
a play in otherness
a way we come
home to ourselves

Breathe into me,
she calls
and your boundaries,
smiling,
dissipate into love itself
"the love we are"
the moon reminds

Beloveds

You know that all are beloved
For all are here to be-loved Being LOVE.

Moon

Greetings Beloved Luna
Fill my body
with your receptive flow
Be that I Am
flowing
into the river of awakening
The dream left me lethargic
and believing in dense
Your alignment with me
lets my coiled up lover
scream freedom
on the rocks
of your horizon
Bleeding me free.
Thank you.

Fondly

Moon full
Hands pulsating
that which empties mind of thought
resonating fiercely
unable to hear when mental chatter
debates the beauty of now
She turns toward Gaia
and fondly
drinks in
sacred blood
by way of magic
Remember gold
has always been gold
she whispers.

Kali ~ Bright Fire of Truth ~ Rage

One day rage visited
I asked it what it was, what it wanted to tell me?
It replied with great force: "**R**eally **A**ngry **G**od **E**ludes"
In response, I questioned what do you need?
The Bright Fire of Truth Herself answered:
"**R**eclaiming **A**ll **G**oddess **E**nergy"

A Way Out

Finding my way
For so long felt
Like a struggle...
In margins of
High school notebook pages read,
"Find a way out"
Years of searching
for something I knew
yet it eluded me,
this way out.
How was I to know?
The way out was in!
Thank you to the signposts of the way,
the awakened ones into which I bumped,
For, gratitude swells
in one who is freed from this struggle
A spaciousness
A heart space
is available within
Those who come can also be free
or at least feel the stirring
of the wings upon their back

The Wild Side

It's just the wild side
but it's still a side
She remembers,
"OK, so I know I have rebelled a bit
But not without guilt or a feeling
of wrong-doing or shame"
Freedom is never birthed from rebellion
It's just the other side of conformity
saying
"I won't sit in your definition of me
your box stifles
so I'll refuse, rebel
I'll fight or medicate
my way out of your box"
Freedom my friend comes
when we surrender judgment
Feel this
when we surrender judgment
Conforming or rebelling
lose their meaning
or a least their power to entice
So when you finish
trying to be who you should be
or trying not to be who "they" want you to be
Be you
It's as simple and magnificent as that

Lack

It arises from the past
Telling you what the little girl felt
When daddy didn't see,
When mom cried at night
When she learned of starvation and war
It jumps from there to here
Promising your belly
That it's not gonna be good
And reminds you
that you were never good enough anyway
It's never good enough,
There is never enough
The illusion mirrors...
How can I be at peace
when the world suffers,
When a child starves,
tsunamis destroy,
when greed rules!
The mind screams...
Nowhere to go but IN...

As We Dance

Where is the pain gone
when I disappear
into You
How can I laugh so loudly
at the apparent atrocities of life
when enveloped in Your love?
I ask
The answer seeps into me
Wordless and without question
as we dance!

Love Is

Squirrel calls again today
To make me smile
The bird flew near in silence
Calling me in
Thank you to those who know
Without a to do list

Attachment

Ego loves to be attached
To that hurt, this resentment
Maybe just to a funny cigarette
Attachment is the ego's way
Of getting you to miss the bliss
Silly ego

Timely Visit

Dancing tears
across
kitchen floor
curled up
sobbing

Aloneness
ignited into Allness
as he whispered
"you my child
have flown the coop"
Sobs to belly laughs
as freedom's wings birth
upon laminate aside the kitchen sink

Ahh dear Hafiz
again and again
you make me
laughing

The Wind

Each morning
let me walk with you
my friend
Let your gentle whisking penetrate
The thickness of my fears,
the density
Of the dream of body
as cage
Instead of magnificent space suit
In which love travels

Let me feel you between the cells
That have fooled me
Into believing in solid
There is so much love
Even when there's not

Love like God
Disguises itself
in what appears not to be itself
For the mere pleasure
Of re-discovering itself...
And you thought you were crazy?

Where Everything Dances

Earthly life
had often seemed a challenge
A kind of bi-polar
manic-depressive existence
Either in heaven or hell
Self-created but nonetheless

And then it happened
I was propelled
to the spaciousness of You
Where only freedom lives
and everything dances

It is nothing you know... space
Nothing you can form
Or explain or even write about
I hoped to be able to share the experience
So I closed my eyes
and I reached out
for You
And word dissolved
into the unbearable pleasure
of the unknowable

Forbidden freedom,
pure potential
Creation itself swallowed me
and just as I was no longer ~
A thought came
that someone was watching
From thought came desire
to share
and thus my journey back
Into me came,

an idea
to share something profound

Nothing is more profound
than the wordless moment
of God's love enveloping you
Can you truly grasp with me
that this is already so
and we were afraid to remember?
It is unbearable the pleasure
and unknowable for the mind... Yes
It is not like the search for God,
the longing ~ All longing disappears
Except when thought came,
a longing to have the people know
and feel it too.

God danced with me again
Conceiving together the thin line
of living truth
of knowing limitlessness
and playing in boundaries
Of being eternal and getting old
Of knowing illusion and living here fully
Nursing a baby and raising a master
Of care of the body and transcending form
Of knowing your oneness
and fully expressing your sovereignty
Of feeling anger and being peace

In the Goddance
everything exists simultaneously
and nothing exists at all.

My Brother's Heart

There she was both bloody and beautiful
beside her a starving child
and upon her back a golden sun

The child's eyes read glory is the sun
and the sun spoke to me
of my ability to respond to world hunger
not later He said, but now

He wrote words that lit the fire in my belly
and all of what is
collapsed into now

My beautiful brother's heart
and his ever-burning question
of what god
would let so many children
starve today
stared me in the face

Any trite answer about the love within
fell completely on deaf ear
until the surge of godDance fire in me said
I don't know what god would
yet now i know
this piece of godness will not

So my friends, lovers, angels and strangers yet,
what kind of fire is in your belly?
for this is the fuel that will feed them

Your fearless alignment
with all that is, yes All That Is
And let love fuel justice

and justice ignite love
and raging wonder
mixed with fierce deliberate action
birthed from collective quantum allowing
for what is So

All of It
to come streaming into the light
of your awareness
so not another night will you sleep pretending
god is somewhere outside of you
and you are powerless

Love is the fierce untamable power
and yes you can
Disappear, go ahead
sleep or be still to merge Yes!

Only to emerge so fully on fire
that nothing in your world can invoke less
than this fierce love and justice
for the people in this maya
of very real flesh and fullness

For when you see love,
and see from love
and when your hands are not afraid to touch
the blood of the wounded
and the swollen belly of the baby girl

And you know, for as you look in her eyes
She sees what you had spent your life looking for
She sees You
God dancing in the eyes of your face
and the screaming mother quiets
as she gently closes her eyes

And you see You
We are on fire now he said
Your belly fire for justice
meets your heart's fire for god
and we together and alone become the 3rd fire[1]

Love in action with every breath, word and touch
It's incredible this honor of action
She calls you

33 ~ Mastery of Love in Politics

Over lifetimes of form
making a career
of making sense
utilizing distraction or intellect
to put some meaning
upon life
and its delightfulness and atrocities
All of it story
Until the day
our tears ignite the fire in the belly
which fans that of the heart
only to emerge as the fire of
life itself
supported fully by the almighty
You dance
Awake. Firm.
Furious passion emerges
from your merging
you know instantly
that all you ever knew is now
only a precursor of yourSelf

---

[1] *From Andrew Harvey, "Sacred Activism"*

in time
if time were so
Mortal in immortality
and presence in the face of distraction
all you are now and will be
making a new career

This day she said yes
Today Marianne Williamson said YES
33rd District, the mastery of love in politics
Every cell of me sang,
as if what I already know
and saw
Is coming home to form
Like an alchemist
living backwards
Always knowing gold inherent within
Even when lead is all you see
She says yes, seeing lead
and evoking the gold
I say yes too

Never underestimate:
Now
The word yes.
what love can really do
how free you really are to make a difference

Always underestimate:
fear
holding back
wishing things were different
doubt

Always know that:
forgiveness frees

brings you home
to where freedom has always been
The power of your authentic Self
breeds love
No matter what.
You do not have to believe it
For it to be so
So it is
Quietly or with a great roar.

You are invited to now
underlying essence of the love you are
always dancing ~ aligning
who you thought yourself to be
with who you truly are
never underestimate:
this true union
The power of love
here-within.

Tonight I asked Hafiz

Where is the love poem
That pulls a heart from a chest
And slams it into god's womb?

I am birthing anew today
Free of who I thought I was

And not yet finding
An "I"
to play in

"That would be it"
He replied.

She Holds Me

Falling in
I simply slide...
The womb of Mother
catches me, saying:
Where have you been
That has taken you
From awareness
of my ever present breast
upon which you curl?

Sounds of Heaven on Earth

The Sounds of Heaven on Earth
are within you
Come,
Dance with me
and we shall sing
your heart's call
and listen
for the one note,
that almost unbearable
joyful tone,
that once heard
will never again
be silenced...

The Search is Over

In succinct steps for years
I searched
Thinking I was looking for You
Shuffling the decks
of tools to access you
Oh Sacred One
All in one moment I disappeared
Swallowed the darkness
And roared wildly
at the mouth of the moon
Still…
This was a square on the chessboard
And I ~ as all that I have ever known
Simply a pawn
at Your table of potential
I no longer search
I Am Yours!

And SHE Loves YOU

I AM Freedom rings in depths
unknown to human minds
where everything dances

The heart of the mother embraces the darkest fear
you thought would destroy
Even your worst act is a cause for Her
To Love You
Love you fully

Love cannot abandon Itself
and never has
that's the real secret

First we Surrender...

Sacred
Unraveling
Releasing
Restriction
Evaporating
Narcissism
Dissipating
Ego
Reality

Into Surrender...

Sweet
Unfathomable
Relief
Rising
Everywhere
Now
Disclosing
Eternal
Reality

The Impulse of Kindness

Today I walked in love
drinking in the sun
birds sang
In a language I am about to know
leaves speak
A tree runs itself in circles
reaching for light
Teaching me of full contentment in being
as I become more

I walk deeper into forest ~
She calls me
I wonder will my heart burst
if gratitude and ecstatic love
expand any more in me
I feel her, my earth Mother
And she smiles

There before me, I see it…
The ever-present impulse of kindness
A branch ~ having loosened from its home base
must have flown from its great trunk
to hook itself in mid air
upon a small tree appearing bare and weak
I can see what must have happened here

As this branch landed gallantly upon her
along came sparrow who began to build her nest
in the branch now perched upon small tree
The little tree straightened herself up
and smiled deeply to be the new home
for a now content traveling friend
and their new guests

Poem

Poem
takes air, love, truth
passion and the unnameable
mixes it with awe
eliciting gasps
from hearts
that know love.

The White Flag Raised

OK my friends ~
that love slows down
beyond fears
fumbling
and before long
tears fall like hail upon your breast

Fists pound calling up from the depths
the desire to be free
Body darts this way and that ~
wondering if it is falling apart
or open

Face flat upon the ground
the white flag raised

Sitting then, tears now fall upon your tongue
Igniting an explosion so brilliant
you no longer think

Hafiz spoke of this
and now you come to know
The goddance is like that you know

Joy

If joy were your only desire
Then everyone
would want to dance with you
Especially the Sun...

Fulltiness

Fullness takes on new meaning
When emptiness is cherished... I promise

Walls

We build them
We break them
We climb them
We shake them
When the walls of armor
Around your heart fall
Breathe and dance fully
So the walls don't return…
Ecstasy is sometimes hard to take

The Mind's Horror Dance

There are some doing the horror dance
Look how bad it's been, or is, or will be
The ego mind calls one to believe
there is a fight to engage in
or something to resist or to try to fix…
Pay a moment's homage to your breath
Let's breathe together now…
Invite God Itself,
Creation Itself to disappear into you
you into Her
For only then will that which you see before you
Be brilliance manifesting itself
In many disguises
Love It All

In the deepest sorrow
The most horrendous horror
I Live, She whispers;
Forgive Me
For being the Source of It all
And in your forgiveness
Exists the bridge to Me
Where your new eyes can see
It is simply impulse in deep contrast
And your Love
Brings Me home

In the Depth

In the depth of winter walks your mother
In the depth of sunshine breathes your soul
In the willingness in your heart God dances
And in the freedom of the wind we smile

Wondering

Wondering as people stop
all the wondering
if that might happen
or wishing this did not
and wonder more
how love will find new ways
of expressing
and how they can dance more fully
for the pleasure of All That Is
I wonder...what then?

The Tune of Love

Limitless love
makes rainbows of lightning
and smiling faces with the stars
Suns waltz to the tune of Love
Calling stars to fall from the sky
Just to get a taste of the freedom
True love brings

God

You are lover, You are trees
You are mountain, You are breeze
Past melts into You and future never comes
You disappear everywhere and only pure love hums

Finally

How many "I've arrived's" does one have
Before she realizes she has never left?

Frees All

From snake skin to lion
from butterfly to soaring eagle
As you shed who you think you are
you can try on any suit to fly or dance
or simply sit a moment.

All of it love in action,
all of it an impulse
that will bring peace

and justice home to now
for all beings.
Can you gift yourself
this freedom that frees all?

We Sit

In times of awakening
sublime states come and go for many,
little moments
of melting into you Beloved.

Nothingness caressing everything
in such fullness
that everything disappears
into nothingness again.

Slowly opening our eyes
here in the darkness
seeing emptiness
falling fully
into the sound
of unbearable delight
emanating
from spaciousness so vast
nothing can define it.

Words certainly limit
when one dances
fully into nothing
as everything comes to Be.
All in the Heart of the Divine
We sit.

Off the Wagon

Perhaps it's not such a bad thing
you know
falling off the Wagon
How did we get on that wagon anyway?
Fall
Feel
Forgive
Free
Finally

Fun & Finally

She, the editor
asked me
"why
the word finally
made it often"
into my writing?

let's see if you can feel it

Have your bones
let go
of your ancestors suffering?
Has forgiveness
bought freedom to your soul?
Is the wall
around your
heart
dissipating?
Is god feeling
closer these days?
Are there more

people who want
food for all and know it's here?
Are there more soul
family who see you
and truths being revealed?

Well, once in a while
as false perceptions
evaporate
some cells in
your universe of body
mind, spirit
may let
out a huge
and utterly
grateful sigh
of relief
Finally!
You know love
as you
We know Love
As All That Is
I Am

If

if you knew in a moment
that all form always changes
would you still hide
so fully
behind
the idea
that you are not
God love
running amuck?

Let Love

In now
love pulses
your blood
your heart
your passions

In now
love guides
your every move

In now
love loves
My love,
let love love.

Golden Mean

Perfect ratios
spiraling
brewing
ingredients
of formless
form
many faces
roots
eyes
wings

May I back up
now
and spin
with you anew?

An Expansion (for Peter & Charlie)

Today as two men
shared
vulnerable
gentleness
truth
resonating from tongues

The feminine
in all life
momentarily speechless
a deep breath
a cosmic sigh

a vulnerable space
so tender
that in it
all are free

Thank you gentle men
for your courage
and return
to love
I AM.

Who

Who is the sunshine
It is you
Who is the moon
you are her too
Who is the wave of the ocean so blue
Who is the dancer of God
It is You

Mooji

The true sage
has to only look at you
calls to now your Self
emerges
the love you are

Who/What you truly are
when the who you think you are
melts away

You do this for me,
In your eyes "I" melt
Emptiness
never felt so full

Loneliness

Emptiness
opens you
Drop into
the place
forbidden
by impending loneliness

Invoke loneliness
to invite you
to the center
of itself

Sit, breathe
Be still and know
I Am
He promised

Love's Resurrection

Resist not what is
my friends
For love, you see, is
the bringer of all things

And in this moment
of love's collective resurrection
so to speak

We are seeing
with our three-dimensional eyes
and feeling in our apparently
dense bones
the unraveling of what love is not

Perhaps you have noticed
within
this resentment or that judgement
more poignantly than before

Or the shame
that tells you
who do you think you are
unworthy one
or guilt screeching
it is your fault you
if only you had done
better yes?

You as microcosm
and dear mother Gaia
as our macro-dimensional
demonstration of love's release
from within

Bubbling up to our awareness
that which had believed
separate from love,
from Source and each other

Perhaps in your English
we call it a byproduct
of an idea
manipulated from
that original perceptual error
A "fall from Grace"

"Smile
says non-resistance
as I
enter your field,
allow what is,
become effortless
a frequency, a flow"

Love is that flow
you are that love
Judge not the guests
love brings up home

When you look with
eyes of resistance
you judge,
or are attached
to what the visitor did
or is now,
you deny love,
extending your visitor's stay

Now that can be
quite a nuisance yes?

So argue not
with what is
"is that so"
is a response that elicits
deep acceptance,
pollinates
a release of
the love hormone
which carries this friend home
to the One heart

You
have new eyes now
and welcome
the apparently personal
or global visitors
For you see
in truth, you now know

"Love relaxes and releases
anything unlike itself"[2]

And Grace
well,
We may call it a
fall **with** Grace
for she has never left you,
She has, and will always,
carry you home
to love.

---

[2] *Louise Hay, "You Can Heal Your Life"*

Fearlessly They Awaken

Fearlessly they awaken
from the long time slumber
the depth of belief in separation
causing listlessness
and lethargy in some
The shared struggle resting
deep in their bones

Despite resistance and fatigue
They gathered, WE gather
Those who can move
Shake the "others'" gifts free

As tears fall
and hands pound upon the breasts
Forgiving each other, yes
Ultimately
Forgiving ourselves
and God, Allah, Yahweh, Ram
For being All That IS
oppressor, oppressed,
abuser, abused, friend, foe.

And We, You and I,
look around the circle
and see OURSELVES
Beyond color, religion, race, gender
Concepts lose their meaning
Thus, we can love ourselves
fully and freely
and your realization of Essence
your wholeness, your authenticity
Frees me.

As Oneness emerges in our awareness
disease dissipates
and competition loses its grasp
and the humans tell Darwin and his friends
where to put "survival of the fittest"
and realize themselves
a species of cooperation
of ONENESS
and dance fully

Supporting the magnificent
Divine sovereign expression
of each being so bright

Walls fall
Wars are paralyzed by the Love
CHILDREN teach
and you and I
Listen
Uniting every cell
home to its Essence
of love
The deep, gentle
fierce and powerful
truth
of who you are are...
Goddess and her beloved
embodied as You

Thank you ~You are the essence of love
in delicious and delightful form
realizing itself free

Supported fully by the Almighty
It is the Goddance for which you have come
I am honored to be dancing with you

一花三二

Master of Freedom

He comes through the ethers
His smile like a knife
That cuts away suffering
Fears and all strife

The love from his heart
blasts open your own
And all of the sudden
You are all alone

In this aloneness
You discover you're free
And laugh at the ideas
Of "my identity"

And now you can see
You become like the Sun
Every Being is free
As you see all as One

If I Danced

If I danced
as wildly today
As my soul desires
Would my body exist
With enough substance
Or togetherness
To kiss my daughter
To sleep
This night?

Gratitude

Feeling deeply the gratitude
Not necessarily for anything
Yet certainly for everything
It's an impulse frequency
this gratitude
That jumps from your heart
Inviting All That Is
to merge with you
This godDance
Is a grateful blissful One

Let Us Gather

In silence, in song
let's all dance along
For time it has ended
In now life is splendid

Become like a child
And stay there a while
Laugh for no reason
Now is the season

We gather in One
Shine like the Sun
The love in your cells
Truth's story it tells

Be here right now
No have to or how
Allow your heart song
That can never be wrong

Awareness

Ahh when the steps to enlightenment
are going to be revealed
the student sits hungry for the way,
paper and pen in hand
Teacher speaks: Step one ~
Awareness
Yes, excitedly the student receives...
Step Two ~ Awareness
"Awareness, again?"
the student questions
Step Three ~ Awareness
Mind fumbles
trying to make sense of this simplicity,
give meaning to it
The soul smiles inwardly
and then bursts out
l
a
u
g
h
i
n
g[3]

Godnight

So it happened again
This time moon stayed for a while
upon my lap
Or perhaps it was I

---

[3] *poem inspired by story told by Alina ~ Oneness Blessing Giver at LA Oneness Event*

Holding her in her sky

I smiled and I danced
found city, home, blue love seat, desk
this pen again
To tell you about it
Fumbling for words that fit

Allness to form
never ceases to amaze. Godnight

Mind Today

Attempted to find
a reason why I was doing nothing
Perhaps, it said, I am lazy
Nope
Perhaps, it said, I am procrastinating
Nope
Perhaps, it said, I should be writing
Silly mind

How can it be divine to do nothing?
To allow your doing
to be spontaneous impulse of godlove?
There is no how, vibrate allow

In this vibration nothing is so very full and life giving
even in the non-movement of stillness
or the wandering around without thought

It felt today like a practice of,
an allowing of what is
without idea of what should be
Be Love

Fly Free

A bird flies
branch, rooftop, nest
Never do we hear him processing
before he can decide
which limb to land upon
And yet are we to hear
two birds arguing
over the best way to go home

In Increments

My friends, the masters of knowing
told me
that for me to know you truly
Would have to come in increments
I see now
How could I ever have believed
what my mind cannot know?
It simply is, they said.
And then I disappeared
Ecstatic grace emptied me
into You
And You into me
Until even the we no longer mattered
How could they have told me?
"You" do not exist!

Prepare

Be prepared for delight
and delight will surface

Your Grace

I wonder if, with the charge your grace allows me
Could I keep on writing as I look upon your face?
The inspiration flowing, pen across the page
A never ending dowry of flowing goddess grace

She dances in my veins, your eyes they pierce my soul
I ask myself who am I, as thought does melt away
Smile as pen invokes, words gently dancing free
Never ending flow of love in which we get to play

Marinated in God Love

Awoke this morning,
body with some aches and pains
My daughter by my side
The first words that came to mind
"All night long we have been marinated in Godlove"
What else would we need today?

Breathe

Breathe attention into your heart
Right now go ahead
Do this for one full minute
or two
an hour
a day?
Life promises you
As you breathe into all stillness
And the gaps between incessant thoughts
Grow
You become the breath itself

The Owl

Look into my eyes, he said
come now, breathe.
I'll meet you in that place
where everything and nothing
dance free.
Where no one owes a thing
to anyone.
And everyone is forever in debt
to love.

Freedom

Searching for it
It eludes
Funny
Its message calls you
Still
Don't go anywhere to find me
Freedom requests
For out there, I am elusive
Inside You
Inside Now
Inside All That Is
I am already so
Fall into me
(and your wings will sprout)

What is YOUR Goddance?

Are you dancing out confusion?
Are you dancing in fear?
Are you dancing your wisdom?

Is your god**dance** not yet clear?
For whether or not
you know it, it's true
The god**dance** is being as You

First notice the step you are presently on
Is it slow or depressed, quick, fast or strong?
With love and compassion
From right where you are
Let the next step be the first
Of your dance to the stars

If you drop from the mind
Right into your heart
Your feet will be moving
You'll know where to start
Nothing in the moment
Would have to change
Accept all that is
as your new dance steps arrange

As you begin to let your
God wings unfurl
Your original dance
takes on new twists and twirls
As you know that only you
Can dance yourself free
As the song of the God**dance**
Only you can be

Many have come
to this life in this form
to awaken the soul
who seemed sleeping so long

Let us join as one song

In many bodies take stance
As one Spirit of love
Each doing our God**dance**!

The Love You Are

You have been asking to wake up, to know love or God,
freedom or peace and happiness. You have longed to be more loving,
rich, thinner, stronger, a better person or wonderful parent.
We promise you, we do not have the tools for fixing. We can assist,
however, in supporting you in loving yourself enough that all that
tells you you are less than love dissipates into love itself, the love
you are. You/we are the ones we have been waiting for.

Peace (for Kathleen)

Peace calls us inward
when tsunamis take our eyes
To horrors of losing everything
that kept this illusion safe and real
Peace calls us deeper
when what we love
transitions quickly
or suffers in body and mind
Peace it promises us
not to make sense of
But to carry us home
when all else fails

On the Edge

Peering over the cliff
bounty and beauty abound

My heart deeply still
I hear not a sound

In corner of mind's eye
fear beckons, what if I'm wrong?
I glance for a moment
There is no wrong in song

My heart it goes first
my head and feet follow
As I dive it's pure love
by which I am swallowed

It Was Me

This one day I stopped
and there You were
I asked, why I had not seen You there before?
You smiled
trees grew from Your head
then a mosaic of faces
moved across Yours
"It was Me," You said,
"you spent everyday with
growing up
It was Me
that birthed you
and birthed from you

"It was Me
that held you
hurt you, fed you
challenged you

"It is Me you nurse,

and mother
and Me with whom
you dance now

"Seen me before?
ahhh yes you have!"

If She Knew

If she knew the truth,
you know,
that she is already free

Imagine the world that she would inhabit
and create

If she knew the truth,
you know,
that she is already whole

Imagine how she would be with him
and them

If she knew the truth,
you know,
That she is already One

Imagine how she'd touch the hearts
and world

Imagine **as she** knows,
You know,
The truth.

Tools

An invaluable tool
For awakening
That is worth its weight
In gold
The invoking,
tending, immersing,
dying to
the Love in all Life
So… breathe love,
Eat love
Dance in love
Cry with love
Write love
Fall into love
Sing love
Meditate on Love
Make love
Stretch into love
Feel loved
And loving,
and lovable
BE LOVE
Try it for a week and see what
H
A
P
P
E
N
S

At Your Beauty

Listening to this moment so fully
past and future collide
Mind ponders
Can I survive?

Seeing this moment so completely
At first glance mind wonders
Will I die
Who is this I?

In this moment everything ceases
As I stand in awe
At Your beauty

As the Moon Suns Within You

She reflects His light
and rides the ebb and flow of existence
She gathers herSelf
from the depths

He, taught to be in control
which meant afraid
She, taught to be less
or careful
or at least nice
He longed for a deeper connection
She longed to be fully
seen and met

He wanted all of her
but was not sure he would survive
She wanted him out of the way

So she could explode into Her allness
Only to have His magnificence
expand just enough
To hold her fully

The dance has just begun
The illusion of separateness dissolving
Where the moon in your womb
meets the sun in your chest
And your wholeness,
so full,
leaves you speechless and
Pure.
Loving.
Powerful.
Present.
Ready.
She opens fully
He enters deeply
They are One
and never the same

As One ~ Mary Magdalen & Yeshua

Drop into the heart of your womb
And call upon Her
She holds the cosmic egg
and frees the pent up bliss
between your legs

Call upon her
and He too will be present
If only to expand
more fully
In Your Magnificence

Being Everything

is simply
resolution with yourself
to resist not the connection
the field of love
the soup of existence in which we move
Fall into
Occupying love
Grace

Get this if you possibly can
The hand of poet
attempts to write bliss
simple motion of pen on paper
is recording this
Bliss Frequency

Breathe it in
We now know privilege to
stabilize this blissful sensation
embodied fully
Sovereignly
Collectively

Resistance speaks only to its pain
and comfort there within
Surrender lays you into chrysalis
Expansion, pleasure
your wings
potential of All That Is
As you,
Delightful you are

Hafiz in Her Love

It may suffice to say his love
is dancing letters into words
across the universe
That come to land
in the hearts of many
Some pine to be
Hafiz lover
Calling forth
the vowels dreaming
consonants
that most delight him
Ecstatic grace pours from the pen
And he weeps words of
the deepest joy
a man could know
He smiles and lays back
again
She asks if she may
serve him an adjective
or verb to allow their
dance to continue
into the night.
She smiles,
when all the sudden
the noun,
the essence of All That Is
swallows the verbiage
along with the tenses
as time and space
disappear
And there he is on a swing
of laughing letters in Her love.

Do You Know

Do you know
that you are
what you dream of?
You are god's delight
You are the wonder
and magnificence of now
You will always be
and nothing you do
or believe yourself
to have done
can take this delight,
this love from now?

When we drop into now
A smile births itself
across my heart
I am reminded,
that you are something
deep and loving
for my soul
and I Am forever
grateful in your
waking

Simply put
love knocks
the answer
matters not
and yet is
always yes
The door is open
unto you

And all you ever

dreamed of
Is
Here Now
How could we have missed
it before?
Rhia said it's just in the box
we did not open yet.
Sweet Sacred Rhia

Listen

Listen to the voices
of our times speak freedom
dogma-less knowing
pouring forth
In flavors meant
only to capture
your heart's realization

No one pretending
to know for you
anymore
No one an expert
in what you
would most delight in creating
but you

Listen to the voices of our times
speak freedom
And share your sound
with us and allow us
to dance
in what we are
yet to know!

Emerging

As Love emerges
reality unwinds its lies
and into your heart
a vision comes

Soon your projection
includes the deep
and utterly
(almost) unfathomable
connection of all life

Breathe my child,
You are Home

~ *From God's Heart* ~

Family

The Privilege

I am the sunshine and the light
I am the freedom of every night
You are the one
You've always known
You are the eagle that has flown
The privilege exists in the choice
To impulse as a girl or boy
A tree, a chair, a bird
An atom that is never heard
All life is deeply content
From God's Heart
It has been sent

The Sun Soaked Clouds

The sun's brilliance streaking
Through the clouds caused my son to say
"Mira mama el poder de Dios"...
Si mi hijo, the power of God
Reflected through the clouds
For all to see
"Become like a child,"
He said

Krishna ~ Eternal Love

Deep love Is
Always Is
No matter what appears
We Know
No matter the space
seemingly in between
We Are
Forever One
and ever honoring
of the gift we have been
and always will be
For One another
I love dancing by your
ever expanding side
You are forever
of my Heart
Catalyst of my
wings
and may you
know love
As You
walking always
gently as you do
upon our Gaia
as your wings
take you places
god
is yet to know
Thank you
Lover of All Life

Isaiah Luis

Before we ever saw you
You spoke from beyond the stars
Of the eternal love we share
Reminded us who we are

Born into our hearts so deep
Your message loud and clear
Your wisdom spoke to me of choice
Home birth, no shots, no fear

I expanded by your presence
beyond what I ever knew
My heart it blasted open
In your love so deep and true

A master of relating
you read people inside out
Wise and warm Isaiah
Your wisdom leaves no doubt

You can always see beyond
And see the better way
A teacher and a friend
A bright and shining ray

In your presence all feel safe
A love so pure and deep
A wisdom strong as earth herself
From your great heart does seep

May you always know your truth
as you play upon this earth
To experience joy and passion
For that you've taken birth

Elijah Luis

Upon the sacred mountain
El Yunque is her name
We called to you sacred son
and into earth you came

From deep within the rain forest
You answered the Heart's Call
From beyond cosmic sun you came
To dance in love for all

Little blessed blissful one
Your joy and light shines
I felt as if my heart was pierced
With your brilliant knowing light

My heart it blasted open wide
As your presence pierced my soul
To bring such power to our world
And remind us we are whole

Your presence in my life has been
a gift of love so rare
And your unique and brilliant way
invites truth and love to dare

You bring out the best in others
Live in integrity and light
I wish for you a life of joy
Of laughter and delight

Unique and pure and loving
A warrior of the heart
Forever I am grateful for
the sacred sun you are

Rhiannon Lakshmi

You make people smile
and stay for a while
you shine like the sun
both sovereign and one

We all knew at birth
Our lives upon earth
In the moment you came
would not be the same

You let the world know
True love you do show
You live in your heart
Each day a new start

Such love you do bring
And make our heart sing
You dance for us all
You answered God's call

Our planet is blessed
and our fears put to rest
As more beings like you
Remind us what's true

We are whole and one
and here to have fun
You teach us with grace
Divine is our race

Souls' Journey in Love

To paint what is so
not seen
I'd paint a rainbow
and brilliant dancing lights
You and Me
Even now
Agreements of the soul
who have danced side by side
in more disguises than one
Willingness to support each other
That Fully
Chris showed me
we are with him now
Not later now
Death of what we think we know,
who we think we are
Into the heart
Aching sometimes, lonely heart
breaking open
the portal to the infinite
calls us
to now
where we are One
this gift we give each other
a catalyst that unravels us
into boundary-less
love
where we know
one another
as All That Is
Love

Zay Meanderings

The feeling
that came over me has never left
The love you opened
inside my heart
the comfort
and deep knowing
That your presence brings

By your side
everyone feels good
The stark and magnificent
honor of being with you
immediately evident
while I held the body
you inhabited
a little round buddha
at 3 days old
Overtaken I felt
the privilege
that was now mine
To share a life beside you
in form

Yet unfathomable,
the feeling of humility, of awe
and gratitude
that I was in this place of honor
to walk by your side.
Those who know you
feel this too.
May you know this
deeply

in your heart and bones
the beauty, power,
love, magnificence
that is you
and the gift your presence is
for All That Is
Like a great mountain
powerful, strong and free
Forever my heart rejoices
in Deep Love for thee
Sacred Sun

Lijah Meanderings

In his presence
All my lies emerge
All the agendas
and things I thought I knew
Lose their grip
Dissipating into truth

At seven he told me
"Mama, think of nothing,
really, really nothing
and then there can be everything,
That's God"
Years later that wisdom seeps
into now

In my silent space
his soul reminded me
of an awareness yet un-owned
"Your freedom is our freedom,"
his eyes pierced.

How precious you are my son
How present I Am is, as You

I remember now what you told me
"breathe mama, we are always here in the oneness too,
you just don't remember."
I remember now

You shine brilliantly
for all
Thank you
Deep love,
Sacred Sun

Rhia Meanderings

The lotus flower calls me
to the memory of Her birth
we dance
This sacred One
A force of nature so pure and powerful
delighted and alive
In awe I am, that I get to play so fully
beside her magnificence
A teacher of presence, joy,
being fully alive
enjoying humanness all the way
She has challenged every sense of myself
so that I melt into more of I AM
and All That Is.
As One,
we dance much more freely
in the now...
I aspire to be like you Rhia
as I grow young.

Rare Family

Blessed I am
with one of those rare families
That stand by you
Nothing that I
or any one of the members could do
Would warrant less than love
Blessed I am
with one of those rare families

Awesome Genes

For each of the always growing
forty something of you, of us
my birth family
every time I think of you
my heart
it smiles
Although it seems the details of your lives
have not always been mine to share in form
My heart knows
it's some awesome genetic yumminess
that leaves imprints upon my soul
the honor to know each
and all of you
to share this bond of love so strong
it withstands
all the craziness
we each can offer
Here or there
quiet or loud
loving who you choose

Each live in the heart
of all of us
In wondrous ways
you rock our world,
we dance fully
together and a-part
thank you.

Rainbows

As the leaves change,
orange, golden rust
Rhia loves the red,
so deep and pretty she says
I think our soul feels happy
to see its brilliance reflected
In leaves of tree,
rainbows we are you know

About the Author:

Judy Guadalupe is called an "inspirer for the soul." This is her first poetry book. She is also published in the anthology, *Pebbles in the Pond, Transforming the World One Person at Time,* and is currently working on a new book, *The Goddance, Dancing Beyond Dogma.*

Judy is a motivational, inspirational speaker, creator and facilitator of Freeing Our Goddance Intensives and Individual Processes. She offers Evenings of Inspiration, Laughter & Love at the Ancient Future Urban Sanctuary in Midtown, Sacramento and at conferences and retreats. Her gift is to inspire and bring humor and lightness to our collective awakening. To find out ways to join Free Your Goddance with Judy, check out one of the websites below.

Judy lives in Sacramento, CA with her family.

Website ~ www.judyguadalupe.com
Facebook ~ *www.facebook.com/freeingyourgoddance*
Children of the New Earth ~
www.childrenofthenewearthconference.com
Seeding the Future Now ~ www.seedingthefuturenow.org
Creating Calm Network ~ *http://creatingcalmnetwork.com/*

Cover Art by Nina Ayzenberg ~ www.ninaayzenberg.com
Editor - Debbie Caldwell in Sacramento

Made in the USA
Charleston, SC
10 March 2016